Westfourth Architecture
New York calls Bucharest

Preface by
Vladimir Arsene

Introduction by
Filippo Beltrami Gadola

WESTFOURTH ARCHITECTURE P.C.,
New York, New York

Vladimir Arsene AIA, UAR, President, Design Principal
ZZing Lee, Senior Associate, Senior Designer
Evan Schwartz, AIA, Senior Associate, Technical Director
John Szabo, Associate, CADD Director
Razvan Carlan, UAR, Senior Architect
Vinu Patel, RA, Project Manager
Miguel Angel Baltierra, Director of Development
Roberto Estorque, Assistant Technical Director
Robert Bettenberg
John Daly Bruning
Young Hee Choi
Anne M. Fletcher
Alexander Jimenez
Son T. Nguyen

WESTFOURTH ARCHITECTURE S.A.
Bucharest, Romania

Vladimir Arsene, President
Cristiana Stefan, UAR, Executive Director
Calin Negoescu, UAR Technical Director
Adrian Ignat, UAR, Senior Architect
Dan Ilie, UAR
Vlad Ghelase, UAR
Camelia Melchiori, UAR
Calin Balasa, UAR
Ioana Isaila, UAR
Mihai Ursachescu, C.E.
Mihaela Mrejeru
Dida Ivan
Diana Serban

Photographers Credits

Vladimir Arsene, John Back, Bernstein Associates,
Photographers. ZZing Lee, Guido Rossi, John Szabo,
Visual Illustration Adrian Ignat,
Visual Illustration by Jelena Erceg, Visual Illustration
Craig Erezuma, Westfourth Architecture

Monograph Team

The materials for this monograph were organized
and edited by Miguel Angel Baltierra
for Westfourth Architecture with the assistance
of Vladimir Arsene, ZZing Lee, Robert Bettenberg,
John Daly Bruning, Younghee Choi,
Anne M. Fletcher, Son T. Nguyen, and John Szabo.

Editorial Director USA
Pierantonio Giacoppo

Chief Editor of Collection
Maurizio Vitta

Publishing Coordinator
Franca Rottola

Graphic Design
Paola Polastri

Editing
Jesse Oona Nickerson

Colour-separation
Litofilms Italia, Bergamo

Printing
Poligrafiche Bolis, Bergamo

First published December 1996

Copyright 1996
by l'Arca Edizioni

ISBN 88-7838-018-0

Contents

York. Bucharest. New York. Bucharest. New York. Bucharest. New

by Vladimir Arsene

A constant wandering between the cities of origin and those of adoption challenges the identity of the immigrant and is conducive to a search for a space in between.

I find it in airplanes flying between my two offices in New York and Bucharest.

It is a paradoxical space in the sense that it permits minimum movement and a complete freedom of mind that can overlap the two worlds that I try to connect. The juxtaposition creates images of a city in which everything converges, nothing fits or has to have a defined meaning and architecture is finally free.

This displacement is confusing. Even more confusing is that we will build glass towers in Bucharest and six story stone and brick buildings in New York. Perhaps we mixed up the whole thing and this is why so many people in both places are confused.

Our towers in Bucharest seem to experience an identity crisis. They are not on a grid (there is no grid) or even in a park, like in the old modernist formula very popular now in Bucharest. (Actually we had some sort of a large park once but we chose to put a big glass cube in it for a film and TV complex.) Or at least the tower could be the end perspective of a major boulevard, another popular formula. (As if the boulevard and the tower were destined for each other by an Everpowerful Planning Authority).

In absence of any zoning or master plan regarding towers, in general we had to set them where our clients have their properties. So these towers are almost hidden, set on tight, odd shaped sites, surrounded by old buildings, in the middle of an elusive "historical district" that is never clearly defined. We figured that perhaps they are a sign of a lively and evolving city.

However they seem to violate a new emerging dream in the city.

That of a coherent and unified Central European type of urbanism, with buildings aligned at the same roof height, with solid street walls so you feel like walking through a cut cake. It is true that Bucharest is a city broken into disparate fragments, that never had a citywide roof alignment program. And it is absolutely not in Central Europe.

"But it is not in North America either," we have been told, "don't enhance the already confused existing urban situation and take your towers back to New York where they belong."

We tried hypothetically, but in New York they are not wanted either. First of all the Star Lido tower is cylindrical and doesn't work with the gridiron.

So we tried to put it on the axis of an avenue (very popular in Bucharest), like the Pan Am building. But it seems that most New Yorkers hate the Pan Am building. Then Lido has a transparent prismatic base that is supposed to be full of life and social activities. "That is totally anti New York!" we have been told. "Have you seen the IBM Building's transparent winter garden? It's full of homeless people at night! We don't like to be observed and anyway, without the old buildings around it, the tower base doesn't make any sense." We tried to bring Bucharest's old buildings to New York, but we experienced serious transportation problems.

So we had to take the Lido tower back to Bucharest.

We haven't been any more successful with the Industrial Export Tower either. We looked for a new site at one of Broadway's intersections with an avenue because the tower has a sharp corner and we hoped that it might fit. It didn't. Besides we have been told that the tower has too many volumes that cling around the central core as if trying to avoid being shaken off by a Romanian earthquake. So why bring it to New York? Again we have been told it was too complicated and it was generated in response to all kinds of site conditions that nobody understands so we should take it back to Bucharest where it belongs.

Besides, there will be no new towers (or as a matter of fact any new architecture in New York for a very long time). So we had to take it back.

We managed to find a place for a single tower, but in Newark, not in New York, where it bothers less people because Newark is in New Jersey. Actually it doesn't fit there either, because although in the city, it's located in the middle of an office complex that recalls a suburban office park, where people travel to and from by car and all caution is taken so that they never have to reach the street and realize that they are in the city. Our tower is too urban, too oriented towards the street, too complex, and on top of everything it contains a Law School on its lower floors.

Speaking of New Jersey. What about the new building for Seton Hall University that we have under construction? This building doesn't fit at all within the officially sanctified postmodern American campus architecture. It has no symmetry, it is the tallest structure on the campus, it's too urban and fails to convince anybody that its construction took place four hundred fifty years ago. Perhaps we should have built it in Bucharest? But it wouldn't have fit at all in the recent city architecture. Not modern enough, too introverted, too boxy and too simple. It doesn't have enough articulation or compositional accents, or features, or something distorted or rotated, and it doesn't look like something just crashed into it.

Speaking of Bucharest. What about the Mindbank Building that we have under construction there? Its program didn't fit on the site.

The site is long and narrow and surrounded by old crumbling buildings. This time an old local ordinance from the 1930s, for that residential area, prevented us from building a tower. We were stuck with six stories to satisfy the roof alignment and the Central European city dream. In absence of any room we had to hide the banking hall below ground, filling the site and creating the largest public basement in the city, and it is known that in Bucharest basements are used for winter storage. On top of that, we had to leave the ground floor void. So there is practically no ground floor.

Can a bank have no ground floor? Perhaps we should have built it in New York on one of those long and narrow parking lots between 14th and 23rd street. It would have fit.

But perhaps those lots are empty because it doesn't make sense to build such oddly shaped buildings.

So it seems that I got everybody upset. The most upset are my colleagues at Westfourth Architecture. They say that I made a mess with this text of all our intense efforts in the past five years.

That I should have talked about contextualism and morphology, about mystery and territoriality, about indeterminacy and transparency, about tectonics and topography, about transcultural fertilization and symbolism, about scale and strategy, about transition and translation, about density and geometry, about tracing and displacement, about technology and poetry.

I think they are confused too. But you may forgive them. They come from seven countries and three continents.

Back to the plane. The movie just finished and the lights are on.

The old gentleman in front of me opens a book that looks like Italo Calvino's *Invisible Cities*.

I bend forward, manage to read above his shoulder, and find myself transfixed:

"By now from that real or hypothetical past of his, he is excluded; he cannot stop; he must go on to another city, where another of his pasts awaits him, or something perhaps that has been a possible future of his and is now someone else's present....."

"Journeys to relive your past?" was the Khan's question at this point, a question which could also have been formulated: "Journeys to recover your future?"

And Marco's answer was: "Elsewhere is a negative mirror. The traveler recognizes the little that is his, discovering the much he has not had and will never have."

The announcement comes. We are landing. I can already see through the window the skyline of the city. It is New York! It is Bucharest!

Introduction

by Filippo Beltrami Gadola

Bucharest and New York. The key to Vladimir Arsene's architecture and design lies in some sort of mysterious bond between these two cities: the capital of Romania, where Arsene received his academic training (and where he has been in charge of the local branch of Westfourth Architecture since 1991), and the capital of the Western world, where for some time now he has been pursuing a successful career, first with architectural practices such as Gruzen Samton or Steinglass and Grad Associates, and then on a totally independent basis with Westfourth Architecture, a dynamic enterprise employing designers from "seven countries and three continents", mainly recruited from Arsene's own students and all involved in an adventure that first began as a sort of challenge at a time of apparent crisis.

This strange bond between Bucharest and New York stems essentially from the overlapping of two worlds, the city where he spent his youth and the place where he first made an impact on the world of architecture. Despite the notable differences in history, culture and tradition between the two cities, to his astonishment Arsene found himself "building glass towers in Bucharest and six-storey stone and brick buildings in New York".

Arsene seems to be both witnessing and actually contributing to the identity crisis that is sweeping through many important cities in Eastern Europe, from Warsaw to Moscow and from Budapest to Tirana. These cities are undergoing quite sudden and disorganized urban development that seems to be totally lacking in any underlying stylistic imprint.

As we might have expected, the usual policy until very recently was to draw in the typological styles and with technical tools experimented with such apparent success in the most progressive spheres of politics, economics and the arts.

Here again the magnetic allure of New York and other huge metropoles in North America seem to have played a significant role, as a utopian model form of urban living which could be successfully introduced (with a different twist) virtually anywhere, in the same way that numerous European cities had tried to copy Paris at the turn of the century.

Arsene's academic background and extensive experience give him that extra edge in tackling the unquestionably intricate question of the potential rebirth and redevelopment of Bucharest.

Significantly, he has not allowed his personal involvement in the issue to blind him in its underlying contradictions: on one hand, the needs and above all expectations of clients and contractors who are still bent on copying stylistic typologies which in many respects are now obsolete and, on the other, the underlying essence and the inherent nature of a city which, despite having been subject to rather brutal urban development schemes in the past, still has not lost its own peculiar *genius loci* and is quite capable of fending off any further attacks.

All this in the presence of an almost total lack of any real planning policy designed to govern and control what could be harmonious urban development and growth.

Returning to his native country, Arsene's architectural work in Romania hinges around a clear understanding of the almost self-evident fact that any new projects must in some way blend in with the existing city. The lack of any real urban grid means that space must be sought in the wide array of housing blocks in what we might tentatively describe as the old city centre: a variety of buildings of different sizes and ages. To quote Arsene himself, the sites were "in general where our clients have their own properties".

It is quite futile to try drawing on traditional Romanian architecture and town-planning for inspiration: the current lack of any real planning strategy and simultaneous reappropriation of private property make it quite impossible to carry out any significant urban-scale development schemes or to insert new buildings in privileged positions, such as landscaped zones or sites overlooking large avenues, as was common practice in the past.

This state of affairs has encouraged Arsene to look for an updated (or updatable) form of urban planning designed to furnish new projects with their own precise identity.

This is the case of the Star Lido Hotel and Conference Center: owing to its size alone, being one of the most important architecture works in eastern Europe; a multi-purpose complex designed to fill an entire block in downtown Bucharest, inserted in an increasingly fragmented urban network in the immediate surroundings of the city's main commercial and institutional structures and, hence, closely knit into the local historical fabric dating back to one of the happiest periods in the city's history.

In Romanian terms, this is a totally innovative project due to both its functional features and the type of people who use it: a luxury residence, first-class hotel equipped with a conference centre and offering services of the highest international standards.

The building's characteristic circular tower seems almost to violate what Arsene calls a newly emerging urban dream, or in other words a "coherent and unified Central European type of urbanism, with buildings aligned at the same roof height and with solid street walls so you feel as if you are walking through a sliced cake".

The circular-shaped design of the Star Hotel makes it impossible to draw any immediate specific cultural conclusions: the building could hardly be described as belonging to the Romanian tradition despite the introduction of an authentic secondary road between the main highway and the building structure, a characteristic of Bucharest's urban grid; neither could it be classed as American or New York-inspired, since it features the kind of transparent basement open to the public which is quite alien to American culture and considered to be an anthropologico-social failure.

Arsene's work in the United States shows the same desire to break free from traditional design schemes. For instance the evident asymmetry of the Seton Hall University Building in New Jersey, which is currently under construction, can in no way be compared to the postmodern style of so-called campus architecture, since it rejects any simplistic temptation to resort to pseudo-historical citation.

There is also a highly intriguing building under construction in Bucharest for the new headquarters of Mindbank, one of the main local private banks.

The size of the long, narrow building lot and the guidelines governing an urbanistic constraint designed to prevent the construction of buildings over six stories tall have resulted in a radically new treatment of interior spaces that is quite unprecedented in either Romanian or classical

American architecture.

The hall where the customer-service counters are located is actually below ground level, covering the entire lot and forming the largest underground space open to the public in a city where, owing to the characteristics of the soil and to the frequent seismic activity, underground areas are usually reserved for storing fuel.

Town-planning restrictions and constraints mean that the ground floor is virtually empty and the offices are located on the four upper floors.

Another important project in Romania is the United Nations Plaza office complex: a service building in the heart of Bucharest which is planned to be built by knocking down some old structures and erecting a sort of eighteen-storey gateway along the main road. The gateway, which is vaguely but quite effectively reminiscent of the Grande Arche in Paris, is clearly designed to offer the kind of perspective views that are such a deeply cherished part of local town-planning and architecture.

The redevelopment project for Piazzale Roma in Venice, an authentic entrance gate to the city facing the mainland, actually dates back to 1991.The construction of a car terminal whose site plan, designed to run along Canale Nuovo and stylistically reminiscent of an upturned keel or sound box of a musical instrument, derives from a careful analysis of Venice's urban morphology. Its regular-shaped grid encompasses all the key points of the city: Piazza San Marco, Rialto Bridge, the Customs Building, and of course Piazzale Roma.

The latest projects, in chronological order, to be designed by Arsene and Westfourth Architecture are centred around Romania, including a new version for the Industrial Export Business Center, which will begin construction this year.

Works

Newark Center for Commerce & Education

Design
Vladimir Arsene for Grad Associates
Architects, Newark, New Jersey

Partner in Charge
Vasant Kshirsagar

Project Director
Steven Carlidge

with
Roberto Estorque, Dante Padilla
Kaushik N. Patel, Vinu Patel, Anne Stich
David Varnish

Model
Gabriel Models, Fairfield, New Jersey

General Contractor
Bellmead Development Corporation,
Roseland, New Jersey

The Newark Center is a hybrid structure which encompasses Seton Hall Law School, covering an area of 18,600 sm a commercial office tower, covering 37,200 sm, and a 1000 car garage.

The project is located in downtown Newark, near Pennsylvania Station and the Pasaic River. The site is bordered by Route 21 (McCarter Highway) and Raymond Boulevard (formerly Morris Canal) to the east and south. The architectural design rotates around the Law Library, the focal point of the entire school. The tower looms up seventeen floors above the top storey of the library, marking the centre of the school and allowing room for future vertical expansion of the Law School collections. The rest of the structure wraps around the five-storey base of the tower, including classroom wings on the north side which are connected by a series of ramps to the faculty wings in the west and south.

The resulting space between the tower and the surrounding school is partly occupied by an "L"-shaped atrium. The atrium, providing the school with a real forum of its own, distributes circulation along its edges across several floors and affords a full view of the library activities.

Top of page, site plan
of building; bottom,
ground floor plan.
Previous page, view
of east facade as seen
from the north-east.

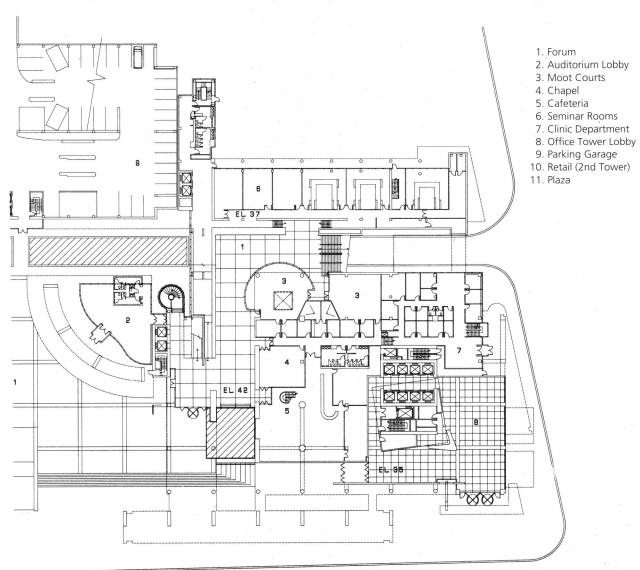

1. Forum
2. Auditorium Lobby
3. Moot Courts
4. Chapel
5. Cafeteria
6. Seminar Rooms
7. Clinic Department
8. Office Tower Lobby
9. Parking Garage
10. Retail (2nd Tower)
11. Plaza

Two views of the
atrium, one from the
north and the other
from the east.

Following page, detail
of the main auditorium.

Night-time view of the building from Mulberry Street.

Community Transit Center

Design
Vladimir Arsene, Rita Ann Burke,
Mihai Craciun, Oreste Drapaca, ZZing Lee
Model
ZZing Lee, Rita Ann Burke

A competition was organized to redevelop Piazzale Roma in Venice, the only site in the city which may be reached by road. The project actually involved the construction of a new bus terminal to be built on the grand canal and the redesign of the entire traffic system.

The designated locations for the terminal platforms had to be surrounded by open shelters and a landscape of urban greenery at the eastern edge of the site. A one-storey tourist facility completed the new project.

Although the project featured essentially small-scale interventions, it also challenged the competitors to design a new "Gateway" to Venice and to address the more complex issue of the city's interaction with the lagoon and the terra ferma. This particular project was designed to create movement along traces revealing a possible matrix for the city's underlying imprint along the Grand Canal. These traces took the form of grid lines on what is potentially a new form of "tracing", superimposed on the map of Venice, defining how the city is geometrically connected to the canal. Designed as a system of bridges marking the transition from the project site to the city, the traces provided the chance to invent real architecture. Reflecting on these archeological connotations, the project transcends the site and emerges through a careful analysis of the topography of Venice. A long wooden shelter running parallel to Canal Nuovo dictated the scale of the site, creating a presence firmly anchored to the city's historical past and caught between the land and the lagoon.

The wooden shelter, which is designed like an old ship or musical instrument, was constructed around a void marking where pedestrian contact with Venice first begins and originating a succession of bridges.

Footsteps and engine noises are designed to create a virtual echo since the shelter is only really a carcass, a pattern of vertebrae that refuses to reverberate.

The bus terminal itself is an oblong-shaped glass building facing the Grand Canal. It mediates transitions between the land and the lagoon, site and city. Its varying degrees of transparency, pulsating to the rhythm of the tide, interrupt the cinematic patterns along the Grand Canal, revealing or implying the space that lies behind.

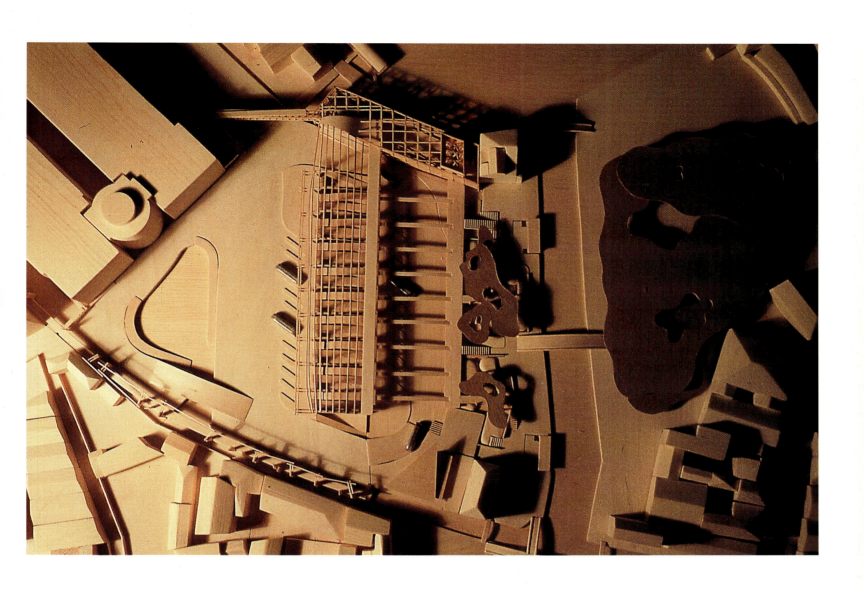

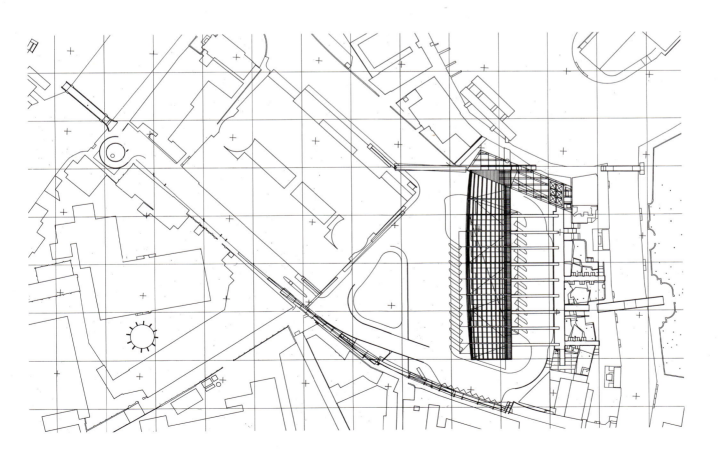

Aerial view of Piazzale Roma in Venice. Below, facades and sections of the proposed architectural structures and view of the model.

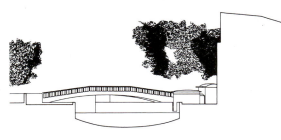

CANAL GRANDE ELEVATION   SCALE 1

SECTION A-A   SCALE 1

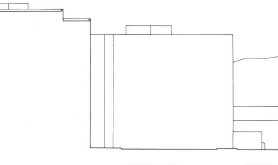

SECTION B-B   SCALE 1

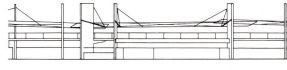

SECTION C-C   SCALE 1

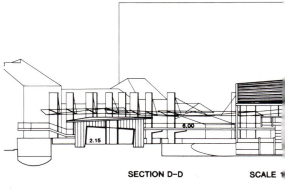

2.15   6.00

SECTION D-D   SCALE 1

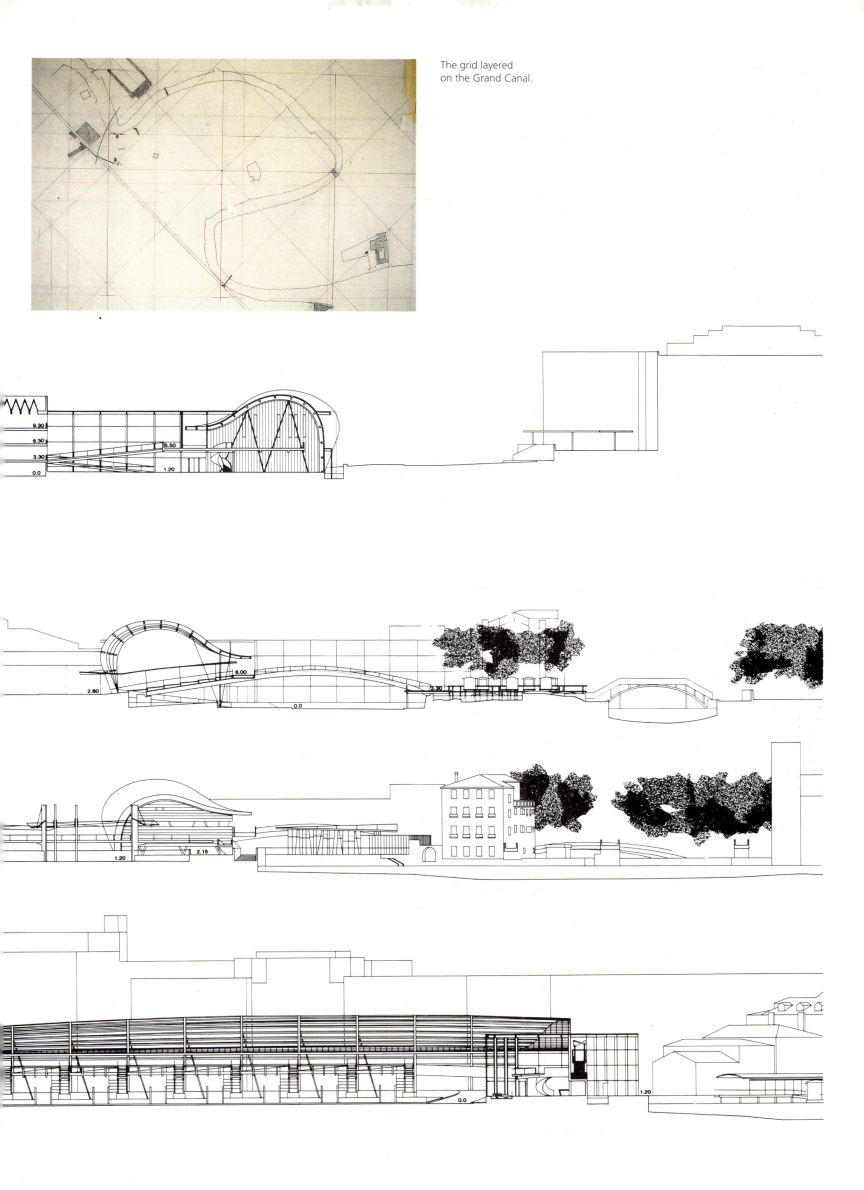

The grid layered
on the Grand Canal.

Industrial Export International Business Center

Design
Vladimir Arsene, Razvan Carlan,
Mihai Craciun, ZZing Lee

with
Oana Bretcanu, Rita Ann Burke,
Adrian Cristescu, Oreste Drapaca,
Roberto Estorque, Michael Horta,
Robert Levi, Calin Negoescu,
Son T. Nguyen, Vinu Patel,
Marius Radulescu

Model
Christopher Rose, Mark Alessi

Consultants
Brownworth Associates, Piscataway,
New Jersey
Consulting Engineers Collaborative,
Kemilworth, New Jersey
IPCTSA, Bucharest

The project site is located in downtown Bucharest, midway between a chain of lakes to the north and the monumental East-West boulevard created as part of the "redesign" of the city in the 1980's.

This area is also an architectural melting pot of modernist mid-rise buildings to the north and low-rise residential developments dating back to the late nineteenth century to the south and west. Several of these landmark buildings are of great historical value and were duly incorporated in the new center.

The real challenge underlying this mixed use development project was to incorporate an office building, 120-room hotel, commercial office space, a TV station and conference/exhibition center on a small pie-shaped site at the edge of the old section of the city.

A single hybrid high-rise "tower" occurs at the intersection between the office building and the hotel facility. The five-storey base housing the TV station and auditorium/exhibition structure wraps eastwards around an existing building, mediating the transition between this 22-storey tall structure and the low-rise buildings to the east.

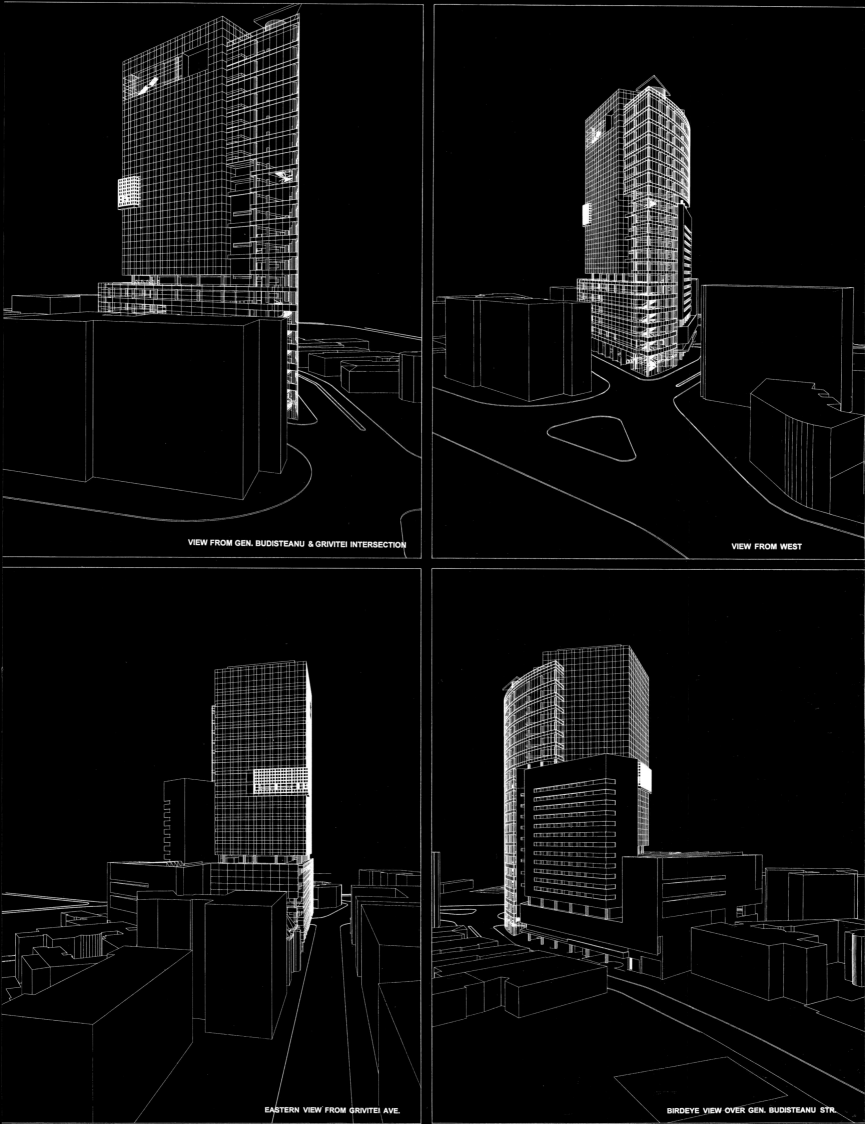

VIEW FROM GEN. BUDISTEANU & GRIVITEI INTERSECTION

VIEW FROM WEST

EASTERN VIEW FROM GRIVITEI AVE.

BIRDEYE VIEW OVER GEN. BUDISTEANU STR.

Site plan. Below, view of the model showing a view of the building at the intersection between General Budisteanu Street and Grivitei Avenue; opposite, standard plans of the hotel and offices.

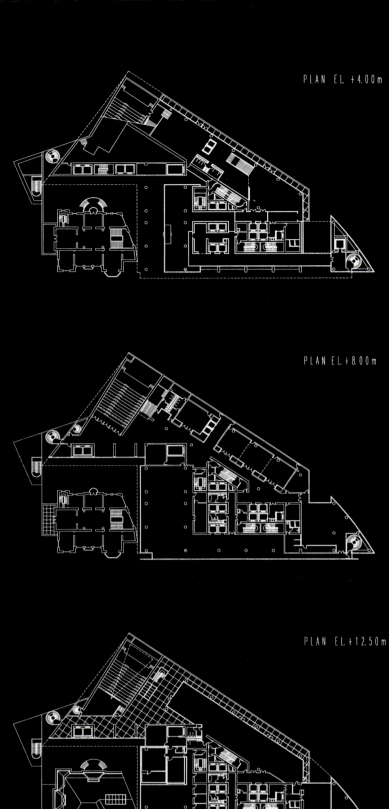

PLAN EL. +4.00 m

PLAN EL. +8.00 m

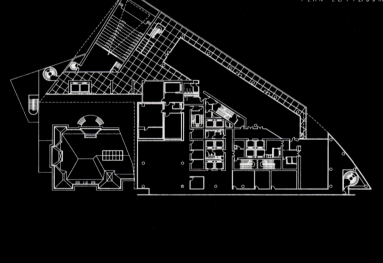

PLAN EL. +12.50 m

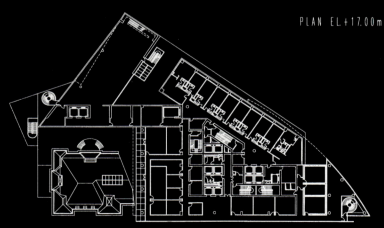

PLAN EL. +17.00 m

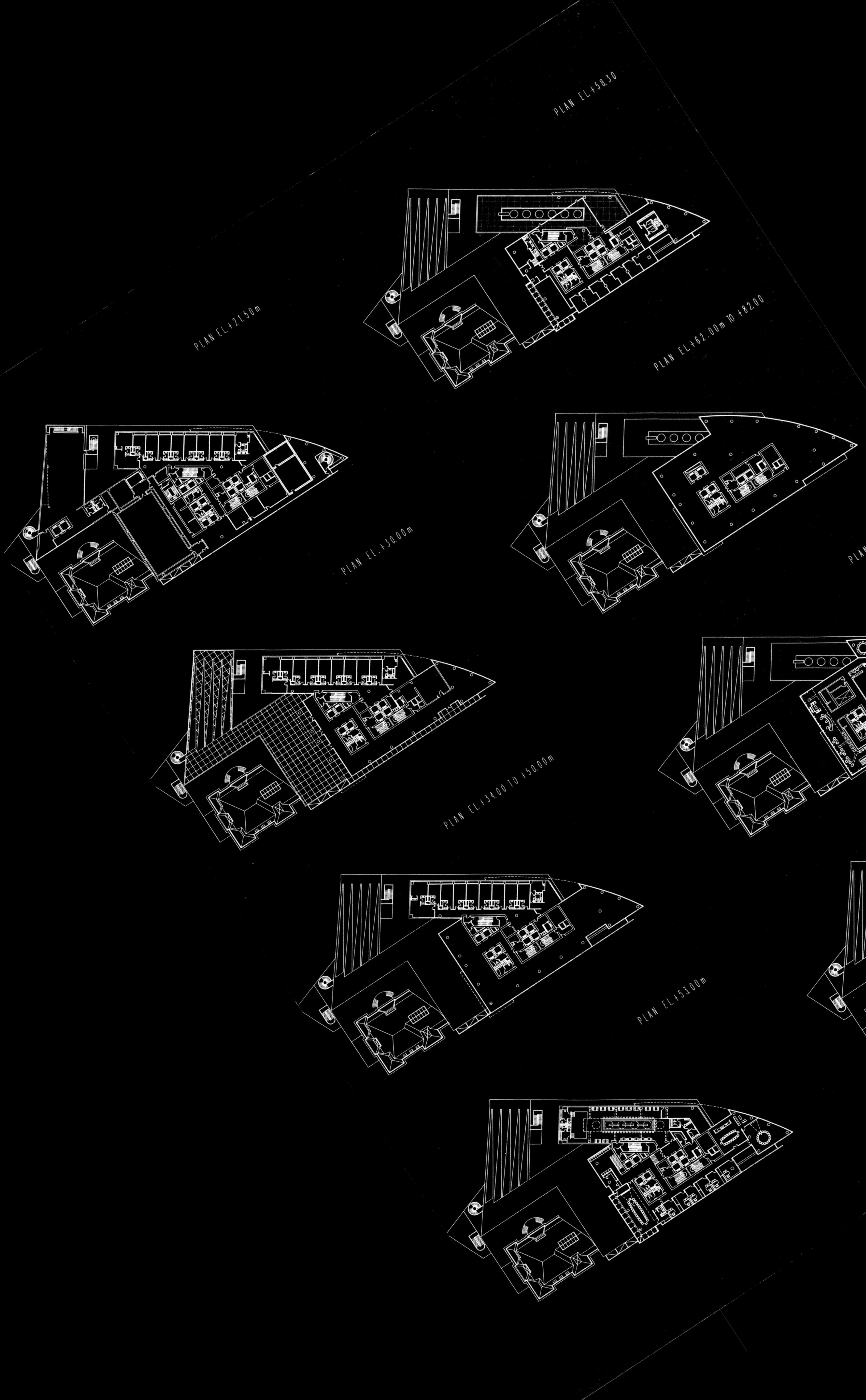

PLAN EL.+58.30

PLAN EL.+21.50m

PLAN EL.+62.00m TO +82.00

PLAN EL.+30.00m

PLAN EL.+34.00 TO +50.00m

PLAN EL.+53.00m

International Center for Film and TV

Design
Vladimir Arsene, Razvan Carlan,
Mihai Craciun, ZZing Lee

with
Darren Corragio, Harry Chambliss,
Michael Horta, Son T. Nguyen,
Marius Radulescu

Model
ZZing Lee

Visual Illustration
Michael Horta

Consultants
Ove Arup & Partners, New York,
New York

The project involved the construction of a new centre for the production of local and international films and television programs, including a new production facility for the Romanian National Independent Television Network, a film studio, and a post-production department.

The flat, irregular-shaped, 23 hectare site in the Pipera district on the northern edge of the city faces open farm land to the north, a residential area to the west, and an industrial development to the south-east. A height limit of 45 metres was imposed by the nearby airport.

The building is designed as a split structure formed out of a cube and a podium. The section of the glass cube incorporates a series of specialist structures, such as a 350 seat screening theatre suspended across the visitors' lobby.

The screening theatre, designed for holding lectures, mass-media debates and live-audience "electronic forums", is expected to be given the status of a "nationally recognized space". Its dark-tinted, glass-panel cladding is designed to allow light to flow through selected sections of the envelope, allowing a mirrored image of the projections to be visible from outside.

The motion picture and main TV studios are located in the central part of the podium. Sloping, landscaped roofs over the adjoining shops and mechanical spaces lead to a large backlot zone to the north and west of the building.

All of the post-production, mixing, studio control, and electronic equipment rooms are situated in a glass-wrapped "high-tech" wing that mirrors the studios along the southern edge of the podium. The flickering lights of the electronic equipment were carefully designed to animate the main south facade at night-time.

Finally, a glazed, triple-height actors' foyer runs along the south edge of the high-tech wing overlooking a linear reflecting pool and entrance court.

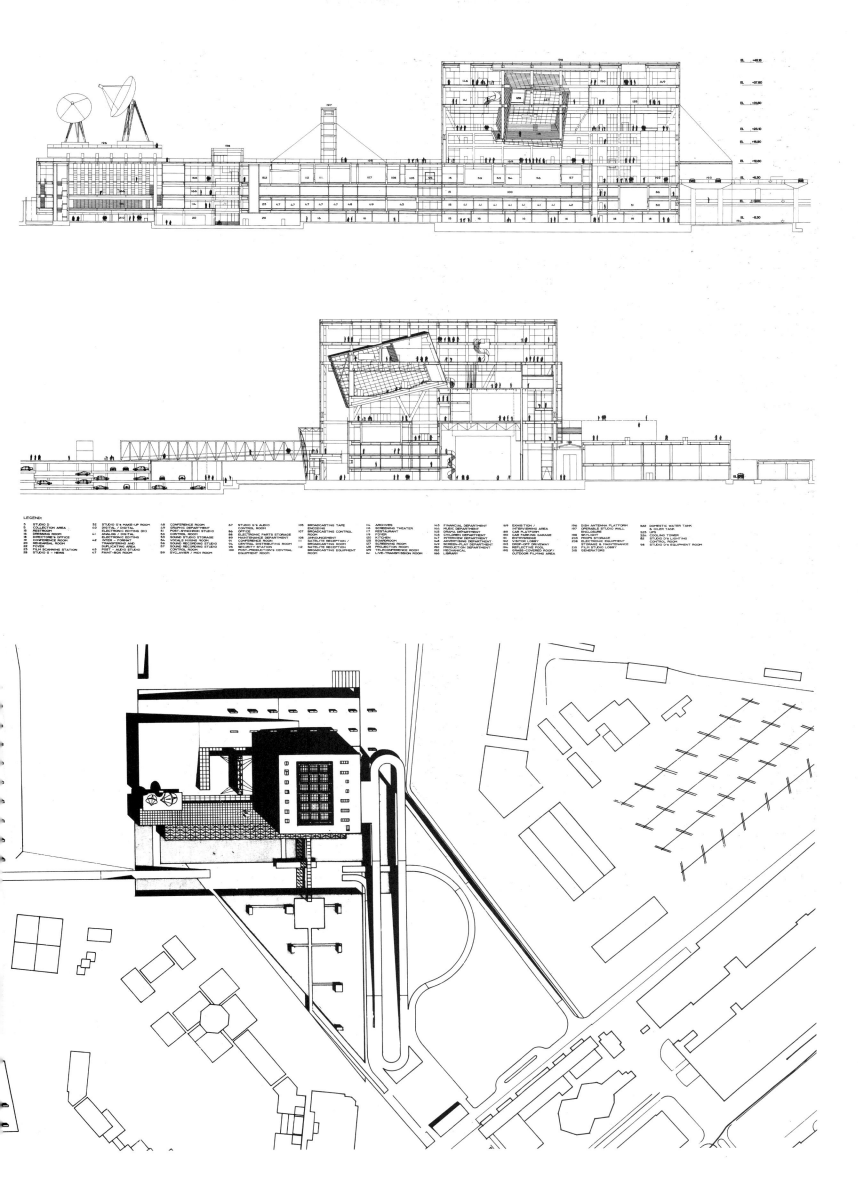

LEGEND:

3 STUDIO D
5 COLLECTION AREA
15 RESTROOM
16 DRESSING ROOM
18 DIRECTOR'S OFFICE
19 CONFERENCE ROOM
20 REHEARSAL ROOM
22 FOYER
23 FILM SCANNING STATION
28 STUDIO G - NEWS

32 STUDIO G's MAKE-UP ROOM
40 DIGITAL / DIGITAL
ELECTRONIC EDITING (DI)
41 ANALOG / DIGITAL
ELECTRONIC EDITING
42 INTER - FORMAT
TRANSFERRING AND
DUPLICATING AREA
43 POST - AUDIO STUDIO
47 PAINT-BOX ROOM

48 CONFERENCE ROOM
49 GRAPHIC DEPARTMENT
51 POST-SYNCHRON STUDIO
50 CONTROL ROOM
53 SOUND STUDIO STORAGE
54 VOCALS MIXING ROOM
56 SOUND RECORDING STUDIO
57 SOUND RECORDING STUDIO
CONTROL ROOM
59 SYCLAVIER / MIDI ROOM

67 STUDIO G's AUDIO
CONTROL ROOM
86 OFFICE
88 ELECTRONIC PARTS STORAGE
89 MAINTENANCE DEPARTMENT
91 CONFERENCE ROOM
95 CENTRAL DISTRIBUTING ROOM
95 SECURITY STATION
100 POST-PRODUCTION's CENTRAL
EQUIPMENT ROOM

105 BROADCASTING TAPE
ENCODING
107 BROADCASTING CONTROL
ROOM
108 ANNOUNCEMENT
111 SATELLITE RECEPTION /
BROADCASTING ROOM
112 SATELLITE RECEPTION
BROADCASTING EQUIPMENT
ROOM

114 ARCHIVES
116 SCREENING THEATER
117 RESTAURANT
119 FOYER
120 KITCHEN
123 BOARDROOM
127 SCREENING ROOM
128 PROJECTION ROOM
129 TELECONFERENCE ROOM
141 LIVE-TRANSMISSION ROOM

143 FINANCIAL DEPARTMENT
144 MUSIC DEPARTMENT
145 DRAMA DEPARTMENT
145 CHILDREN DEPARTMENT
147 INTERVIEW DEPARTMENT
148 ADVERTISING DEPARTMENT
149 SCREEN-PLAY DEPARTMENT
150 PRODUCTION DEPARTMENT
152 MECHANICAL
166 LIBRARY

169 EXHIBITION /
INTERVIEWING AREA
189 CAR PARKING GARAGE
190 CAR PLATFORM
191 ENTRY-BRIDGE
192 VISITOR LOBBY
193 DROP-OFF DRIVEWAY
194 REFLECTIVE POOL
195 GRASS-COVERED ROOF/
OUTDOOR FILMING AREA

196 DISH ANTENNA PLATFORM
197 OPERABLE STUDIO WALL
ENCLOSURE
198 SKYLIGHT
208 ELECTRONIC EQUIPMENT
STORAGE & MAINTENANCE
210 FILM STUDIO LOBBY
315 GENERATORS

322 DOMESTIC WATER TANK
& OILER TANK
323 UPS
324 COOLING TOWER
82 STUDIO D's LIGHTING
CONTROL ROOM
98 STUDIO G's EQUIPMENT ROOM

Bucharest, Romania
1993, under construction

Mindbank Headquarters Building

Design
Vladimir Arsene, Razvan Carlan,
Mihai Craciun, ZZing Lee, Son Nguyen,
Roberto Estorque (New York), Adrian
Cristescu, Calin Negoescu (Bucharest)

with
Adrian Cristescu, Andrew Donaldson,
Roberto Estorque, Alexander Jimenez,
Son T.Nguyen, Dante Padilla, John Szabo
and Calin Balasa

Model
Christopher Rose

Visual Illustration
Craig Erezuma

Consultants
Structural Engineer: Proconstruct SA,
Romania
Mechanical Engineer: Roinstar SA,
Romania

Builder
Italimprese Spa, Rome

Construction work on the headquarters of one of the largest Romanian banks, located on a narrow strip of land in one of the most architecturally prestigious districts of the city of Bucharest, began in January 1995.

The importance of the project site lies mainly in its close vicinity to the city's main commercial centre in an area that is planned to be integrated into the downtown business district.

The site is actually bordered by a six-storey apartment block to the west and a four-level structure, housing part of the Romanian Academy archives, to the east, both built in the 1930's. The houses and workshops on the other two sides are all basically one-storey buildings. Owing to the peculiar characteristics of the 2500 square-metre site and in response to both spatial requirements and zoning constraints on the width of the ground floor area, the architects designed the main bank hall 4.80 metres below ground level, despite Bucharest's notoriously poor soil, the high water table, and strong seismic conditions.

This scheme allows the site parameters to be exploited to the maximum and guarantees optimum security for banking operations. Its single floor distribution also simplifies circulation and creates a highly representative space for one of the most important institutions in the Romanian financial world.

A series of parallel events unfold on the ground floor, which opens up across the northern section to create a double-height space allowing daylight to flood into the public area. The back offices of the banking hall are naturally illuminated through a peripheral skylight running along the entire length of the southern section. The rest of the banking functions are distributed across three other floors above ground level, leaving a fourth floor, accommodating a small cafeteria and library, free for future developments.

The corridors on the upper floors are made of glass panels affording views of the overhead skylight and the building's main wall is clad with Romanian limestone panels, as is the south facade. Vehicles travelling along a suspended "floating" bridge interact with pedestrians to create a sense of horizontal motion that plays against the vertical movement of the escalators, grand staircase and elevators.

The building's main structure is constructed out of a two-directional moment-resistant concrete frame, incorporating large columns because of Romania's strict anti-seismic code.

A closely packed set of friction piles have been used to construct the basement wall, at the same time providing the surrounding buildings with extra protection.

The overall design strategy is intended to transform an old turn-of-the-century residential district into a more business-oriented neighbourhood as part of an attempt to modernize the city's traditional urban matrix.

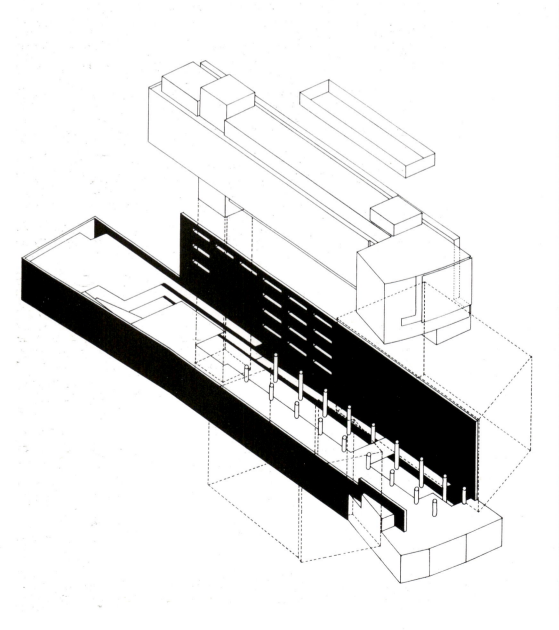

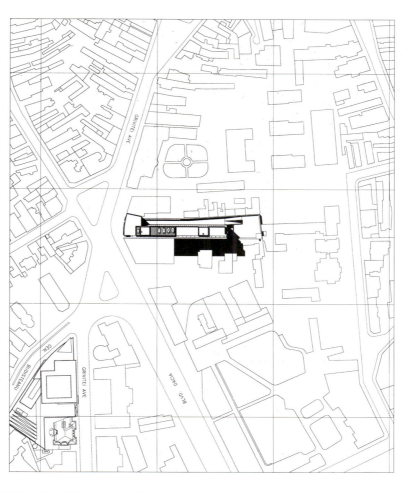

Previous page,
the model seen from
above and exploded
axonometric drawing.
This page, site plan and
another view of model.

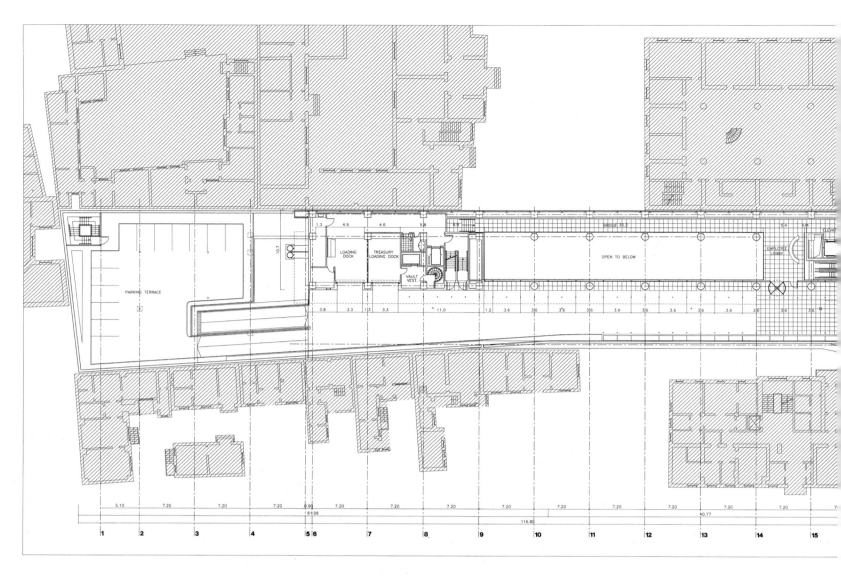

PARKING TERRACE

LOADING DOCK TREASURY LOADING DOCK

VAULT VEST

OPEN TO BELOW

BRIDGE 35.2

EMPLOYEE LOBBY

ELEVATOR

10.7

1.3 4.9   4.6   5.8   8.9

3.8 3.3 1.3 3.3   * 11.0   1.2 3.6 3.6 3.6 3.6 3.6 3.6 3.6 * 3.6 3.6 3.6

5.10   7.20   7.20   7.20 0.90 7.20   7.20   7.20   7.20   7.20   7.20   7.20   7.20   7.20

67.06
116.80
40.77

1   2   3   4   5 6   7   8   9   10   11   12   13   14   15

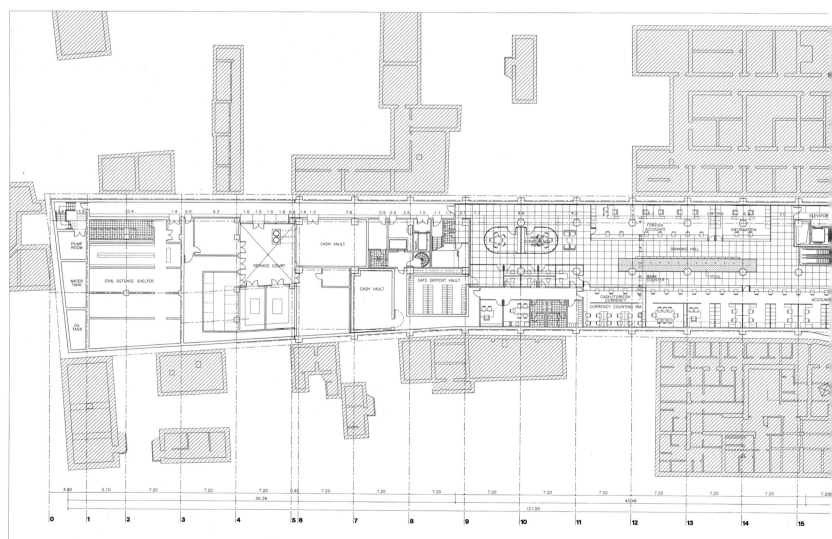

PUMP ROOM

WATER TANK

CIVIL DEFENSE SHELTER

OIL TANK

SERVICE COURT

CASH VAULT

CASH VAULT

SAFE DEPOSIT VAULT

FOREIGN ACCOUNTS

CONFERENCE ROOM

CASH/FOREIGN CURRENCY

CURRENCY COUNTING RM

BANKING HALL

INFORMATION

BANK COUNTER

POOL

ACCOUNT

ELEVATOR

10.4   1.4 0.9   6.3   1.6 1.5 1.5 0.8 1.5   7.8   0.9 0.9 2.6   1.5 1.1   9.6   4.2   0.9 0.9   3.0

4.80   5.10   7.20   7.20   7.20 0.90 7.20   7.20   7.20   7.20   7.20   7.20   7.20   7.20   7.20

50.39
121.00
45.48

0   1   2   3   4   5 6   7   8   9   10   11   12   13   14   15

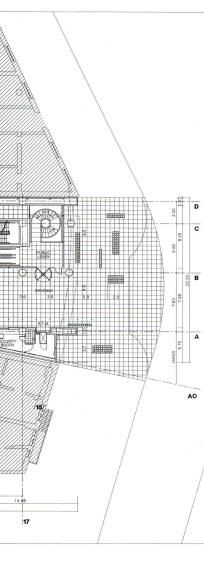

Top, ground floor plan; bottom, banking floor plan. Below, rendering of cross section/elevation facing south.

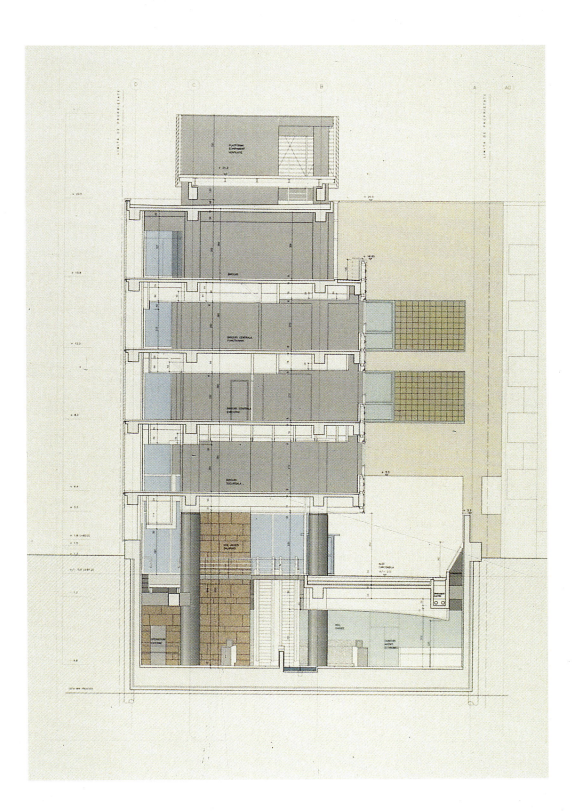

View of the building's work site. Following page, computer rendering of south elevation.

East Windsor Pre-Kindergarten

Design
Vladimir Arsene, Razvan Carlan,
ZZing Lee, John Szabo
Model
Andrew Donaldson

This project involved the design and construction of a 10,000 sm. headstart facility for low income pre-school children and their families.

The site, which covers an area of approximately 1.5 acres, lies in East Windsor, New Jersey. It actually stands adjacent to land owned by the Peddie School (an independent co-educational secondary school), although the two properties are divided by a stream flowing behind the site. The site is easy to reach just off one of the town's main streets, nearby the New Jersey Turnpike.

The new facility is actually designed to take up half of the buildable space, positioning the five classrooms and playground so that they face south-east and the parking/access area towards the north-west. The site's topography derives from the building's volumetric definition.

The repetitive module reiterates throughout the project facilities, a deliberate transition from a building to a site-oriented strategy designed to cater to future developments. The module mediates between a three-dimensional pre-manufactured element and a matrix unit, providing structural flexibility and versatile mapping for any given site.

The set of five smoothly flowing roof modules over the single-storey building allows for greater height and enables natural light to flood into the classrooms and multi-purpose room.

The building is planned to be enveloped in clapboard siding and painted flat-seam metal roofing.

The cone-shaped roof framing that opens towards the playground to the south-east creates a secondary volumetric classroom arrangement towards the north-east. This configuration breathes life into the classroom space and fosters a heightened perception of daylight transition and motion.

The main structure has a wooden frame constructed out of ASI (stress-rated lumber flanges and structural wood panels) and LVL (laminated veneer lumber) beams for roofs.

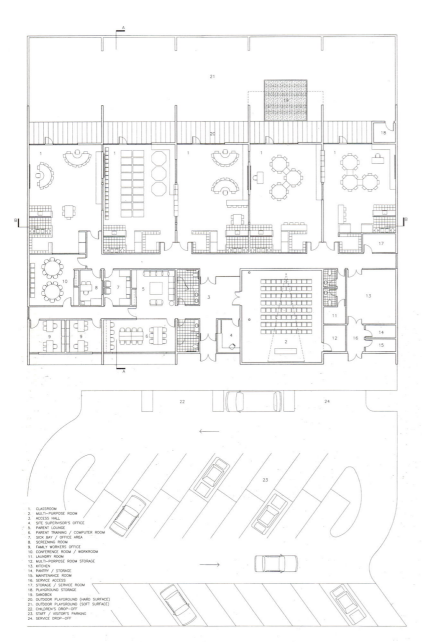

Floor plan showing
the functional layout
of the building's interior
spaces. Below, general
view of the model.

1. CLASSROOM
2. MULTI-PURPOSE ROOM
3. ACCESS HALL
4. SITE SUPERVISOR'S OFFICE
5. PARENT LOUNGE
6. PARENT TRAINING / COMPUTER ROOM
7. SICK BAY / OFFICE AREA
8. SCREENING ROOM
9. FAMILY WORKERS OFFICE
10. CONFERENCE ROOM / WORKROOM
11. LAUNDRY ROOM
12. MULTI-PURPOSE ROOM STORAGE
13. KITCHEN
14. PANTRY / STORAGE
15. MAINTENANCE ROOM
16. SERVICE ACCESS
17. STORAGE / SERVICE ROOM
18. PLAYGROUND STORAGE
19. SANDBOX
20. OUTDOOR PLAYGROUND (HARD SURFACE)
21. OUTDOOR PLAYGROUND (SOFT SURFACE)
22. CHILDREN'S DROP-OFF
23. STAFF / VISITOR'S PARKING
24. SERVICE DROP-OFF

The Star Lido Hotel and Conference Center

Design
Vladimir Arsene, Razvan Carlan,
ZZing Lee

with
Robert Bettenberg, John Daly Bruning,
Younghee Choi, Mihai Craciun,
Roberto Estorque, Anne M. Fletcher,
Alexander Jimenez, Son T. Nguyen,
Evan Schwartz, John Szabo

and
Adrian Cristescu, Canelia Melchiori
Cristiana Stefan, Vlad Ghelase

Model Builders
Alexander Jimenez/Westfourth
Architecture, Bucharest
Tenguerian Model Concepts, New York,
New York

Visual Illustration
Jelena Erceg, Craig Erezuma

Photography: John Back, John Szabo

Consultants
Consulting Engineers Collaborative,
Kenilworth, New Jersey
G + W Associates, New York, New York
Roinstar SRL, Bucharest
Walls Design Associates,
Douglaston, New Jersey
Ricci & Co., New York, New York
Emanuel Necula Engineers, New York

The 82,000 sm Star Lido multi-purpose hotel complex is designed to cater to executive business travellers and the upscale conference/convention market. The Lido project also encompasses the largest hotel/conference complex in Romania, right in the heart of downtown Bucharest.

The new Star Lido hotel complex features a twenty-eight-storey cylindrical tower housing the guest rooms built on a six-storey base containing the main hotel facilities and public Conference Centre. The 133-metre glass tower constitutes a new landmark right at the hub of the city's overall concentric topography. Its six-storey glass base knits into the surrounding urban fabric like a transparent three-dimensional living room, drawing on a new typology of architecture to enhance its civic role as a public space.

The cylindrical tower is clad with a partially blue-green curtain wall, while the curved balconies are enclosed in an unsealed clear-glass curtain wall to facilitate the circulation of air and prevent condensation from forming.

The building's main structure is made of a reinforced concrete circular shear wall core fitted with reinforced concrete support frames made of columns and beams. There are also a series of perimeter basement walls to transfer seismic forces through to the foundations system.

The main entry to the hotel is through a special plaza at the southern end of the block, and the drop-off driveway is covered by a glass canopy.

Inside, vertical circulation is provided by a series of elevators running up to the guest rooms, penthouse suites, and luxury apartments. Two sets of escalators also serve the Ballroom and Conference Centre. Entrance to the parking facilities is via a garage ramp that wraps around the central tower core and joins together the two underground parking levels. The valet-serviced parking lots can accommodate 235 cars.

This huge realestate project is designed to initiate a new phase in the city's evolution, further embellishing its modern downtown centre dating back to the 1930's. At a height of thirty-five stories, it is also one of the tallest structures to be built in Eastern Europe.

Plans of first
and ground floor with
Lido Concourse.

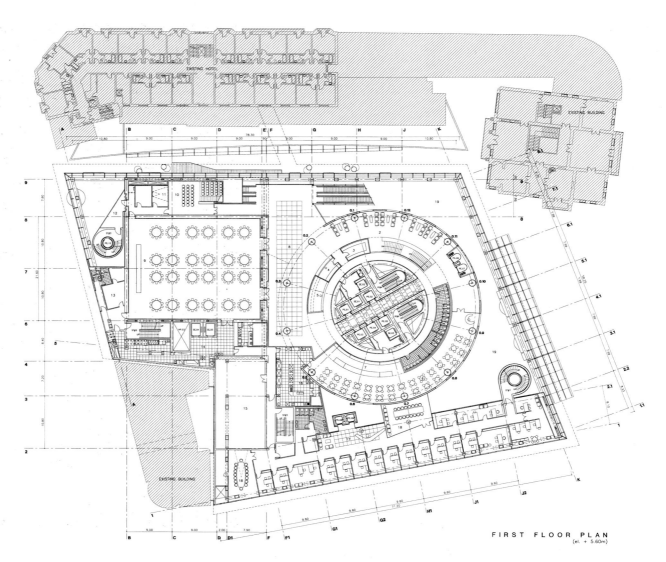

FIRST FLOOR PLAN
(el. + 5.60m)

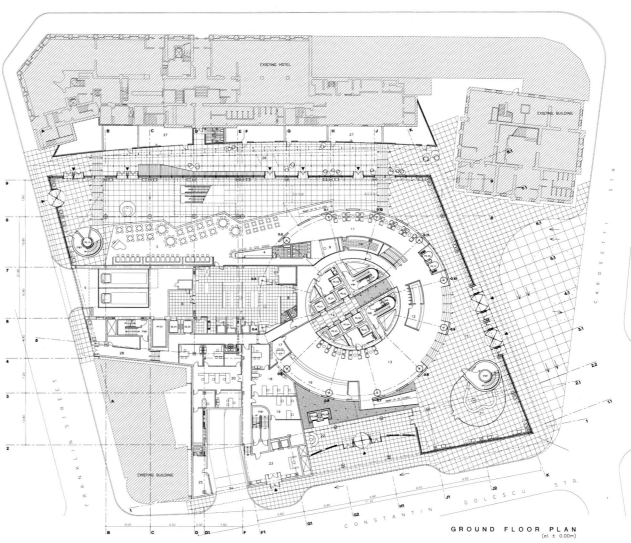

GROUND FLOOR PLAN
(el. ± 0.00m)

Model view, looking
north, of entry Plaza
at the corner
of C.A. Rossetti Street
and Constantin Golescu
Street, and typical
section.

In this page, panoramic
restaurant floor plan
and, below, east
elevation. Opposite
page, model view of
north-east corner of
basement.

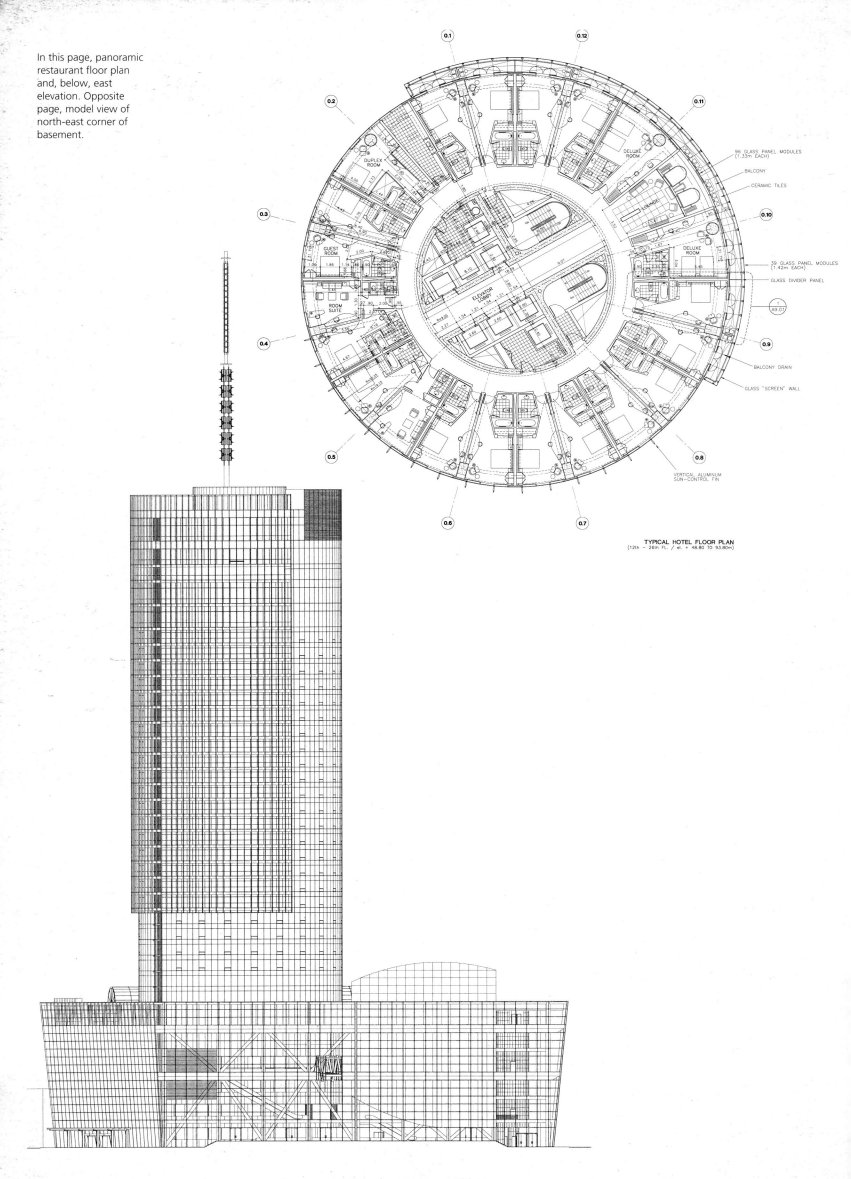

96 GLASS PANEL MODULES
(1.33m EACH)

BALCONY

CERAMIC TILES

39 GLASS PANEL MODULES
(1.42m EACH)

GLASS DIVIDER PANEL

BALCONY DRAIN

GLASS "SCREEN" WALL

VERTICAL ALUMINUM
SUN-CONTROL FIN

TYPICAL HOTEL FLOOR PLAN
(12th – 26th FL. / el. + 48.80 TO 93.80m)

NAPIER UNIVERSITY L.I.S.

In this page, view
looking north-west of
model. Opposite page,
view looking south
along the retail gallery.

Computer rendering
view of south facade
area as seen from
the west.
Opposite page, detail
of the model.

South Orange, New Jersey,
1995-1997

Seton Hall New Academic Support Building

Competition Team
Vladimir Arsene, Younghee Choi,
Alexander Jimenez, ZZing Lee,
John Szabo

Project Team
Vladimir Arsene, John Daly Bruning,
Roberto Estorque, Anne M. Fletcher,
Alexander Jimenez, Vinu Patel,
Evan Schwartz, John Szabo

Design/Builder
Torcon Inc.

Model Builders
Tenguerian Model Concepts, New York,
New York

Consultants
Consulting Engineers Collaborative,
Kenilworth, New Jersey
Hacbnl - Civil Electrical Engeneers,
Princeton New Jersey
Shen Wilson & Wilke, Acoustical,
Audiovisual System consulted.

This was the winning design in a competition for a new Academic Support Building at Seton Hall University in New Jersey. The new building will be used by the School of Business, the School of Education, and the Department of Psychology. It will contain approximately thirty classrooms and a 350-seat auditorium.

The compact site strategy under this six-storey structure placed at the northern edge of the campus green serves to create a heightened sense of place and acts as a defining catalyst for a disparate cluster of campus buildings and open spaces.

The minimal footprint left by the new building means that the rather scarce areas of landscaping are left intact, while its height provides a proper edge to the campus green.

The 118,000-sm building accommodates teaching areas in both the basement and ground floor levels.

This facilitates the access for students and also allows the auditorium to be used separately for campus events. The second level hosts the Undergraduate Department of Psychology, the Department of Professional Psychology, and the Family Therapy Unit. The upper three floors hold the College of Education, Human Services, and the Business School. All three departments are arranged around a central interior court that provides a gathering place for faculty and students.

The atrium configuration of the upper floors bestows a distinct sense of identity on each of the wings that wrap around it.

A centralized circulation pattern encourages inter-departmental and inter-school interaction, promoting a sense of community for the building's occupants. While the top three levels revolve around the atrium, the lower two floors define the campus greenery, as the building is simultaneously focused inwards and oriented towards the University grounds. The main facade is clad in Mankato jet mist limestone and marble.

The other facades are clad in dark shades of Ironspot brick.

This page, plans
of the upper and lower
teaching levels.
Following page,
longitudinal section
looking north and plan
of the third floor
accommodating
the undergraduate
department
of psychology, and
the department of
professional psychology
and family therapy.

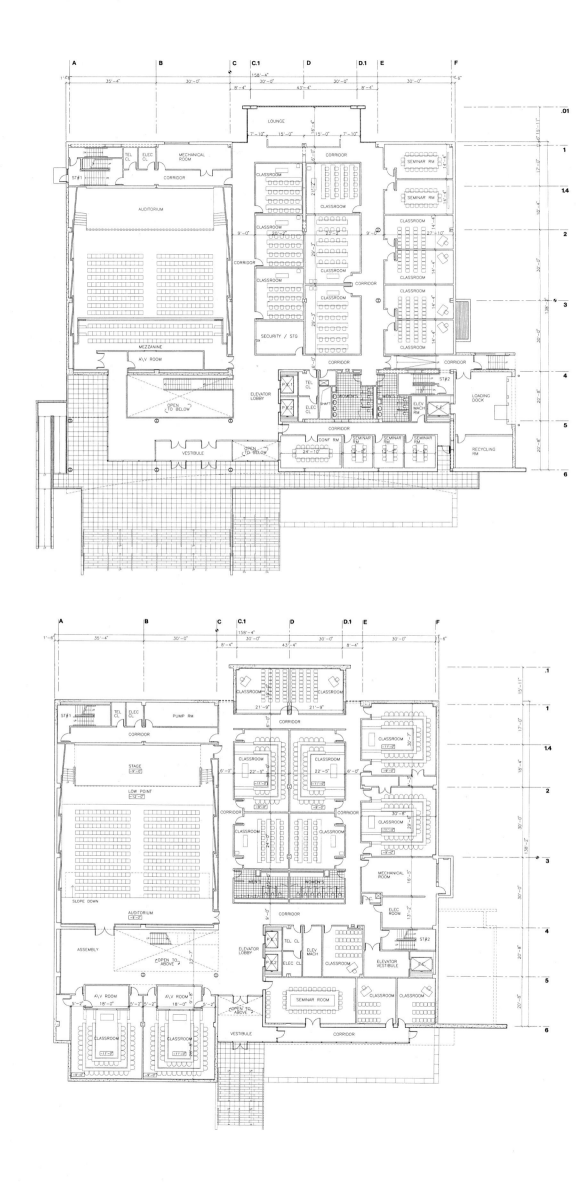

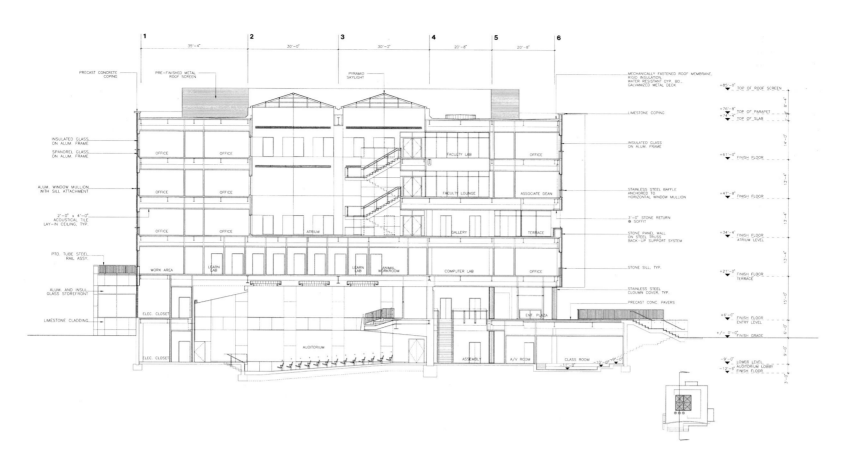

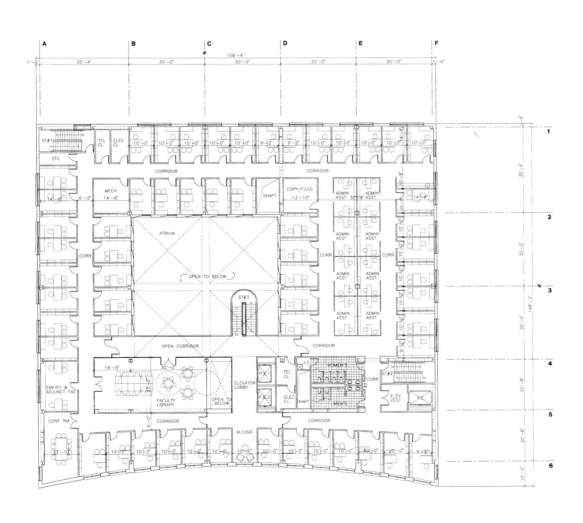

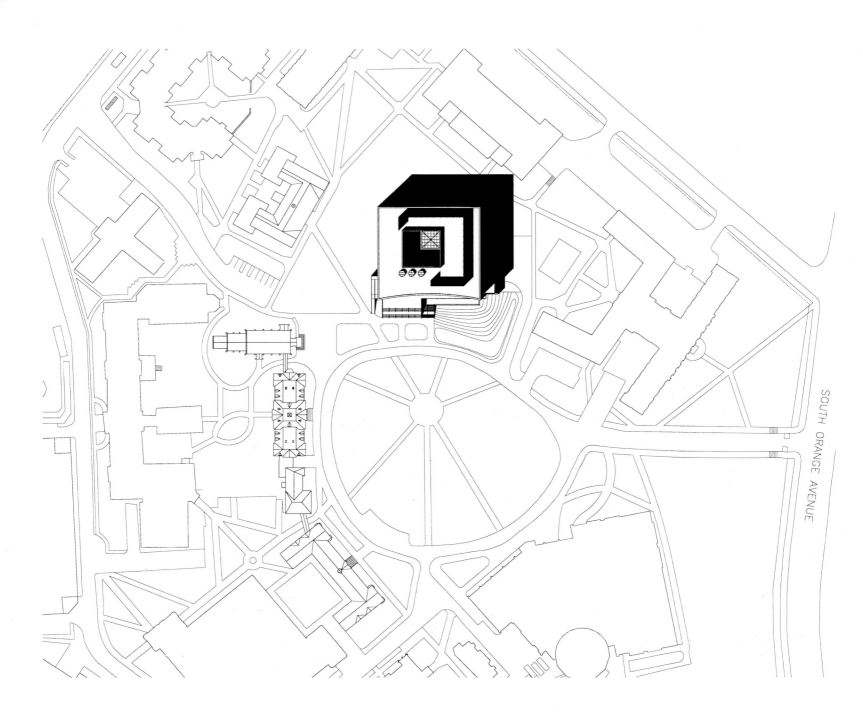

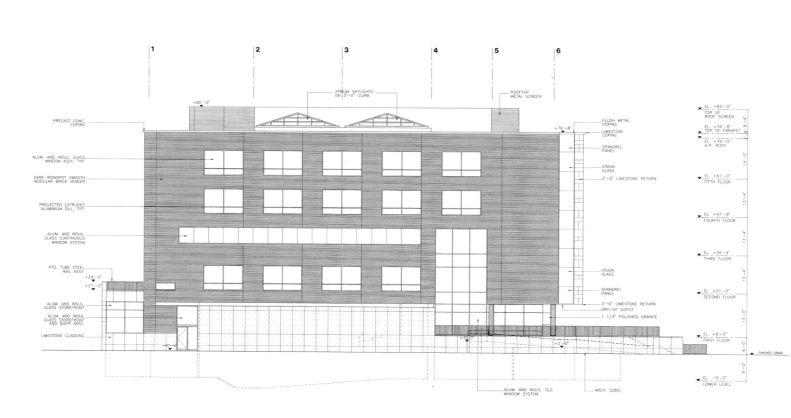

ATRIUM SKYLIGHTS
ON 3'-0" CURB

ROOFTOP
METAL SCREEN

PRECAST CONC.
COPING

FLUSH METAL
COPING

LIMESTONE
COPING

SPANDREL
PANEL

ALUM. AND INSUL. GLASS
WINDOW ASSY, TYP.

VISION
GLASS

DARK IRONSPOT SMOOTH
MODULAR BRICK VENEER

3'-0" LIMESTONE RETURN

PROJECTED EXTRUDED
ALUMINUM SILL, TYP.

ALUM. AND INSUL.
GLASS CONTINUOUS
WINDOW SYSTEM

VISION
GLASS

PTD. TUBE STEEL
RAIL ASSY.

SPANDREL
PANEL

ALUM. AND INSUL.
GLASS STOREFRONT

3'-0" LIMESTONE RETURN
DRY-VIT SOFFIT

ALUM. AND INSUL.
GLASS STOREFRONT
AND DOOR ASSY.

1 1/4" POLISHED GRANITE

LIMESTONE CLADDING

FINISHED GRADE

ALUM. AND INSUL. GLS.
WINDOW SYSTEM

ARCH. CONC.

EL. +85'-0"
TOP OF
ROOF SCREEN

EL. +76'-8"
TOP OF PARAPET

EL. +75'-0"
H.P. ROOF

EL. +61'-0"
FIFTH FLOOR

EL. +47'-8"
FOURTH FLOOR

EL. +34'-4"
THIRD FLOOR

EL. +21'-0"
SECOND FLOOR

EL. +6'-0"
FIRST FLOOR

EL. -9'-0"
LOWER LEVEL

Previous page, site plan
and south elevation.
Below, view of
the sitework and east
elevation.

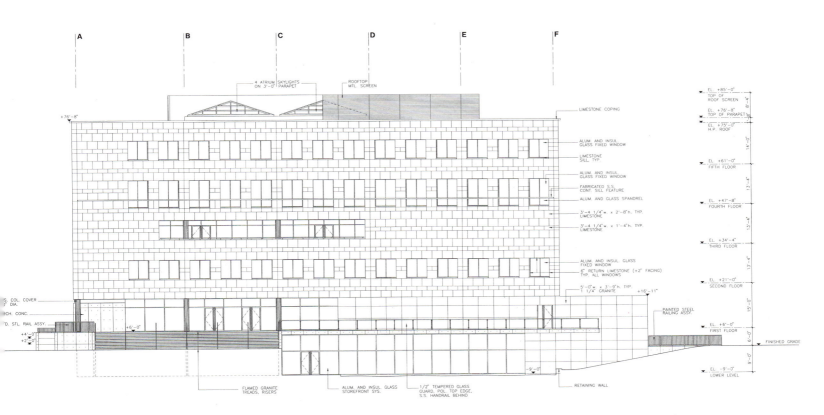

EAST ELEVATION

Craiova Sports Complex

Design
Vladimir Arsene, Son T. Nguyen,
John Daly Bruning

Model
John Daly Bruning

The project for this new multi-purpose sports facility is designed to upgrade the city of Craiova's existing soccer stadiums.

The old stadium will be completely redesigned to attract international sport events by increasing its seating capacity in close agreement with international safety standards.

A 140-room hotel is planned to be built alongside the new ground. Every single hotel room will afford a panoramic view of the playing field.

Two restaurants, a conference centre, an exhibition space, and medical clinic will be accommodated in the upper levels on the north side of the complex. Retail space, a press club, and management offices will all be located beneath the grand stands.

An olympic-size swimming pool, built on the lower level, is designed to widen the range of sport facilities available. A clerestory above the swimming pool offers visitors a foretaste of the main complex before entering the wider arena of the soccer stadium.

The maximized structure enveloping the entire building, cleverly designed to mirror the site's asymmetrical boundaries, actually conceals a carefully orchestrated arrangement of interior facilities.

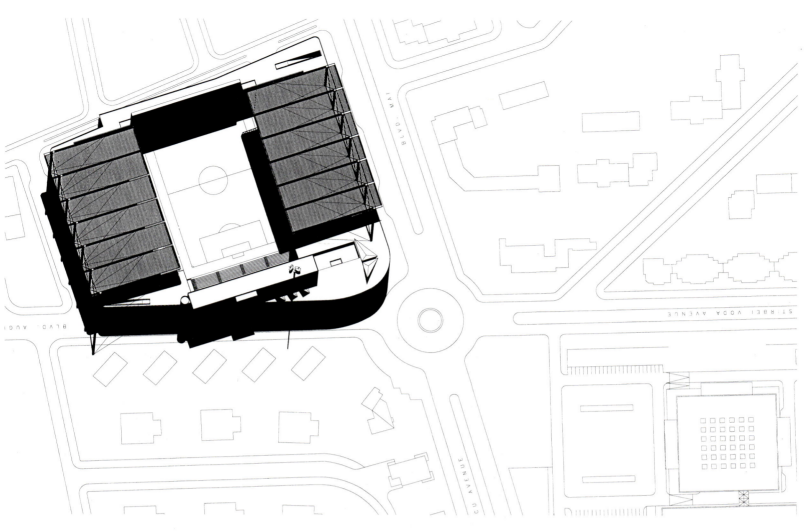

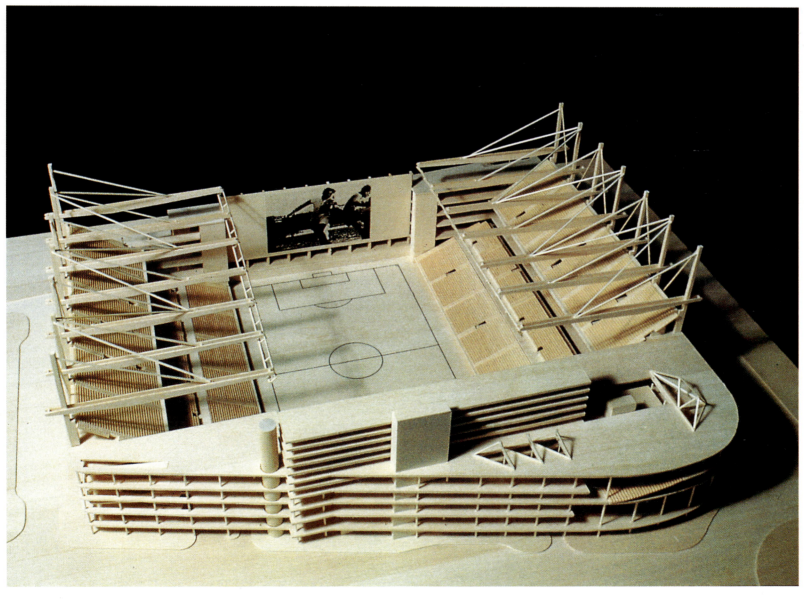

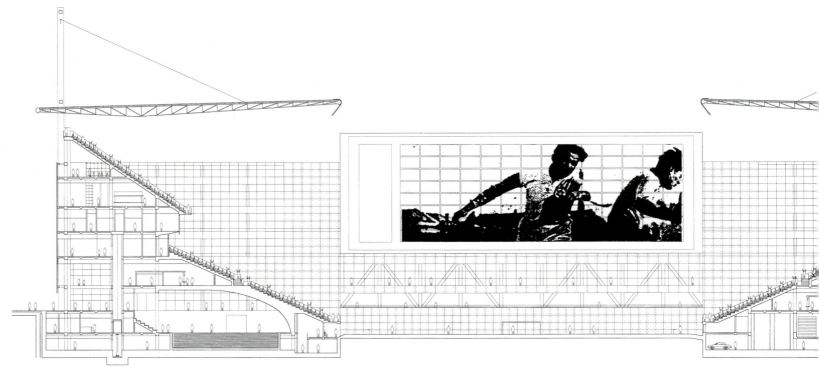

Cross section looking
west and, opposite,
view of the model
looking from the north-
west towards the main
retail entry at the
intersection of May 1st
Boulevard and August
23rd Boulevard.

United Nations Plaza Office Complex

Design
Vladimir Arsene, Robert Bettenberg,
ZZing Lee

Model
John Daly Brunning

Visual Illustration
Craig Erezuma

The site of the new United Nations Plaza in downtown Bucharest is close to the Dambovita River, near the city's main boulevards, monuments and business plazas.

The project involved the demolition of some old buildings, originally designed for residential use, and then the erection of a single eighteen-storey "gateway" structure, whose top eight levels will span over United Nations Boulevard.

A second-floor sky lobby , affording spectacular views along the river banks, is designed to connect the two lower wings and facilitate vertical circulation. A pair of escalators and a monumental stairway lead up to the lobby and two special elevators for the disabled link it to the two ground-floor entrance halls. Each wing is also equipped with express elevators to connect the sky lobby to the top nine floors of the building.

All the office space is carefully designed to provide spectacular views of the river, to reduce the plenum space of ducted fresh air, to increase the floor-to-ceiling height, and to accommodate flexible renting of well-equipped offices.

The top eight floors contain the highest quality offices offering the best views and the slickest facilities, including mechanical, electrical and communications pathways with raised floors for additional data cabling.

The loading docks are located at ground level, while the technical-maintenance areas, including the boiler system, emergency generator, water/oil tanks and pumping stations, are all below ground level in the basement.

The two-storey underground parking facility is designed for both office workers and the public at large.

Careful consideration was given to the suitability of this site for commercial uses before it was decided to convert the old structures into this new state-of-the-art office complex in downtown Bucharest.

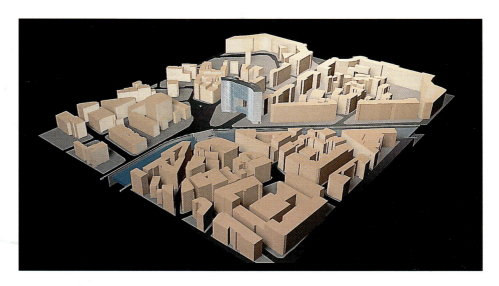

This page, from top
down, plans of top
office floor, standard
office floor, mezzanine
floor and ground floor.
Opposite page, main
elevation and computer
rendering of complex
as seen from
the east along United
Nations Blvd.

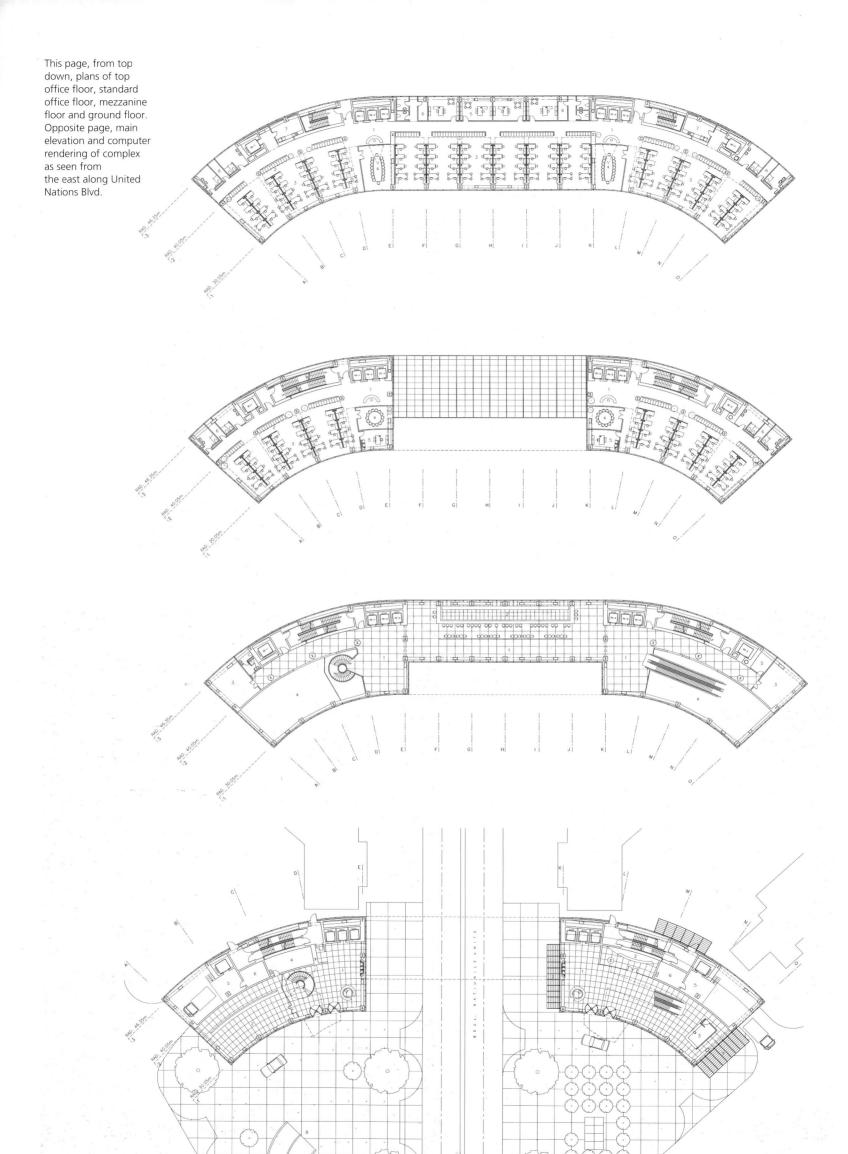

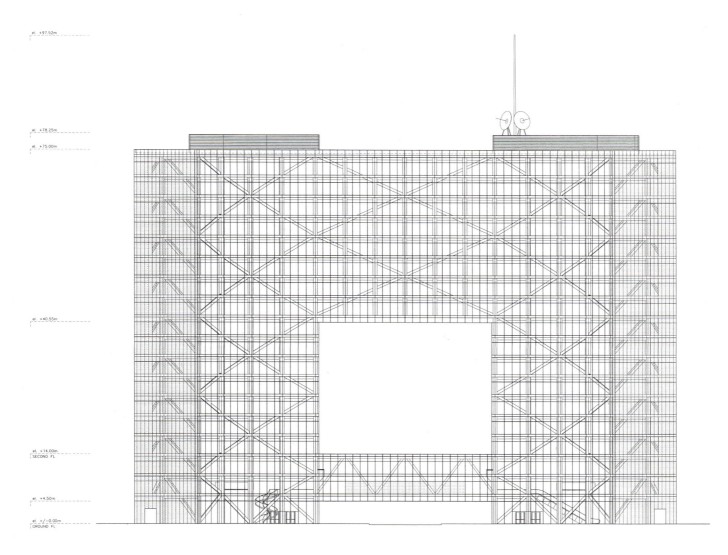

Craiova, Romania, 1996

Craiova Sports Arena

Design
Adrian Ignat,

with
Adrian Cristescu, Calin Negoescu,
Ioana Isaila, Mihai Nuta

Visual Illustration
Adrian Ignat

Alteration and modification work on the Craiova Sports Arena was devised around its old reinforced concrete structure that remained intact after a devastating fire in 1994.

The arena's seating capacity was increased from 2000 to 5000 seats by extending the old spectator stands.

The relocation of functions involved the total separation of public spaces, VIP services, press facilities, and the areas reserved to athletes.

The public entrances are on the east and west sides of the building, providing access through a series of annexes accommodating cafeterias, cloakrooms, and toilet facilities.

These annexes are located under the multi-purpose playing field. Access to the stands is available via four flights of stairs at the corners of the arena.

VIP services, such as special entrances, foyers, meeting rooms, and annexes reserved for VIPs and sport officials, are located on the west side of the arena in an interchangeable prefabricated steel structure.

Athletes' facilities, such as lockers, warm-up rooms, training facilities for track and field events, medical services, administration offices, and technical areas, are all located in a separate building connected to the main building by a bridge at the same level as the playing field.

The TV broadcasting rooms and offices and other press facilities are spread across the upper floors of the building to guarantee direct views of the playing field.

The arena roof is built of steel trusses running in a north-south direction. A spectator standing on the west side can be dismantled to allow the arena and its roof to be extended in the direction of its west-side boundary.

The old arena and its new extensions are all contained inside a perimeter glass enclosure supported by a steel structure.

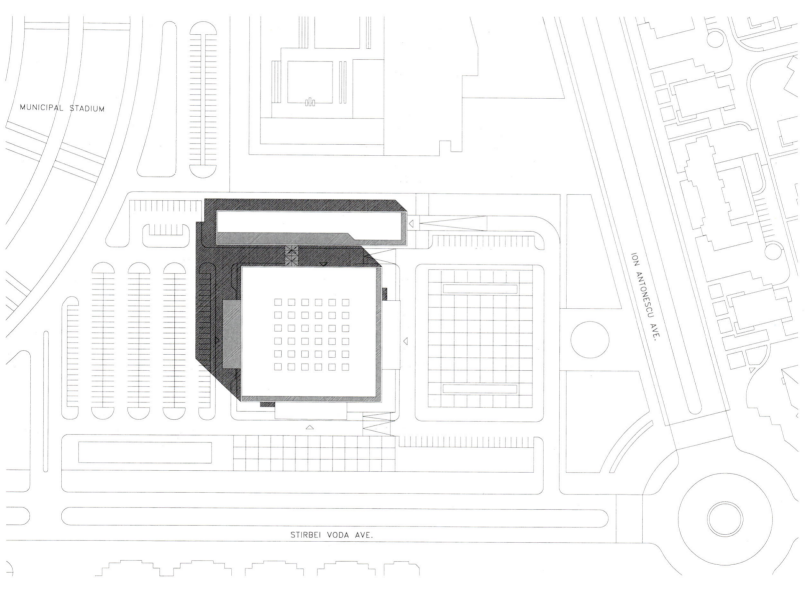

MUNICIPAL STADIUM

STIRBEI VODA AVE.

ION ANTONESCU AVE.

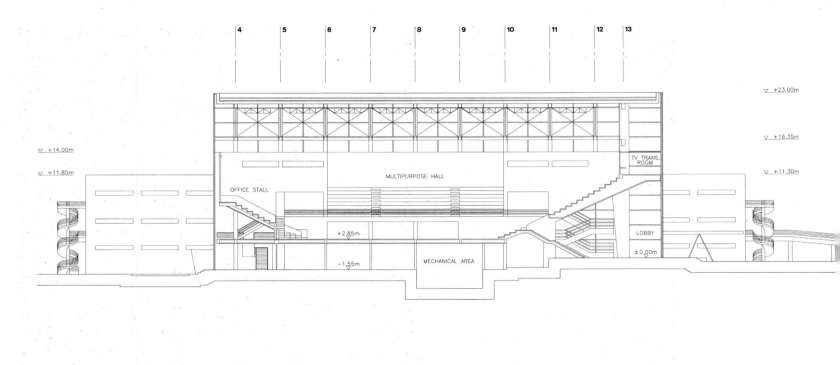

| | | | | | | | | | | |
|4|5|6|7|8|9|10|11|12|13|

▽ +23.00m

▽ +16.35m

▽ +14.00m

TV TRANS. ROOM

▽ +11.30m

▽ +11.85m

MULTIPURPOSE HALL

OFFICE STALL

LOBBY

±0.00m

+2.85m

−1.55m

MECHANICAL AREA

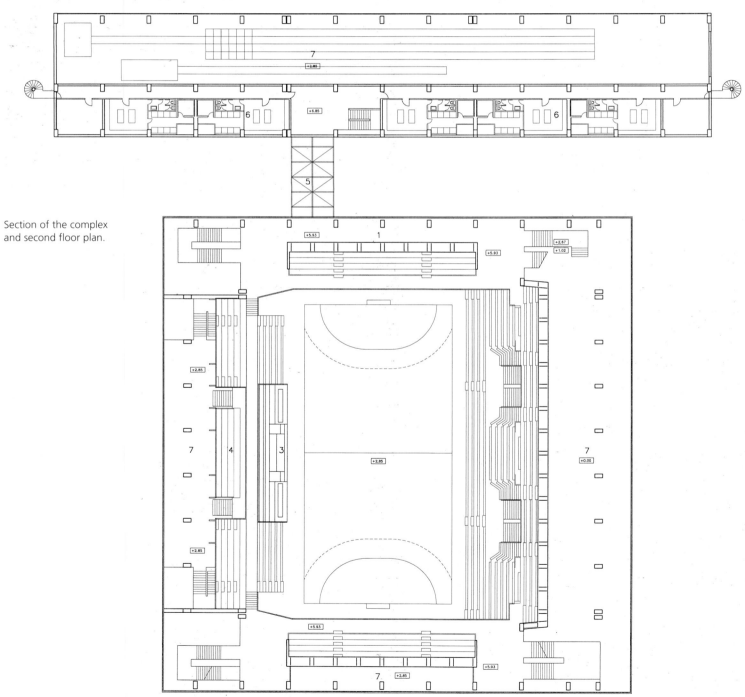

Section of the complex and second floor plan.

Two computer-rendered views of the building.

Installation
for the artist Ion Banulescu

Design
Vladimir Arsene, Rita Ann Burke,
Darren Corragio, ZZing Lee, Andrew
Piedl, John Szabo

The installation for the "Centauri:
Knight to Queen Nine" exhibition at
the New Jersey Institute of Technology
School of Architecture, 1992,
presented sculpture works by the artist
Ion Banulescu.

Views of the installation
highlighting the
interaction between
architectural space
and museum exhibits.

Biography

Professional Activity

since 1991 Westfourth Architecture, P.C., New York, President

1983-1986 Grad Associates Architects, Newark, N.J., Senior Associate, Senior Project Designer

1986-1987 Gruzen Samton Steinglass, Architects, New York, Principal Designer

1978-1983 Abramovitz-Harris-Kingsland, Architects, New York (formerly Harrison & Abramovitz), Senior Designer

Academic Activity

1988-1995 Adjunct Professor, Studio Critic New Jersey Institute of Technology Newark, New Jersey

1994-1996, 1990- 1991, Adjunct Professor, Studio Critic Pratt Institute School of Architecture, Graduate Program Brooklyn, New York

1990-1992 Visiting Professor, Studio Critic Pratt Institute School of Architecture International Architecture Seminar Summer Program

1987-1989 Adjunct Professor, Studio Critic New York Institute of Technology School of Architecture Old Westbury, New York

Building (1980-1996)

Star Lido Hotel and Conference Center
Bucharest, Romania
Design 1994-1995
Construction 1996-1999

Seton Hall University Academic New Support Building South Orange, New Jersey
Design 1994-1995
Construction 1995-1997

Mindbank Headquarters Bucharest, Romania
Design 1993-1994
Construction 1995-1997

Seton Hall Law School, Newark, New Jersey
Design 1987-1989
Construction 1990-1993

Newark Center for Commerce & Education Newark, New Jersey
Design 1987-1989
Construction 1990-1993

The "Regatta" Apartment Building Battery Park City, New York
Design 1985-1986
Construction 1986-1988

Elizabeth Police Headquarters & Municipal Court Building
Elizabeth, New Jersey
Design 1985-1986
Construction 1986-1988

School of Atmospheric Science
Miami, Florida
Design 1983
Construction 1983-1984

Crowley House,
Glen Head, New York
Design 1983
Construction 1984

Jacobson & Wilder Agency
Design 1983
Construction 1984

Fitzgerald House,
Flemington, New York
Design 1984
Construction 1985

American Electric Headquarters
Columbus, Ohio
Design 1980-1981
Construction 1982-1984

Projects (1980-1996)

1995 Seton Hall Law Dormitories, Newark, New Jersey

1995 Corbeanca Residential Development, Bucharest, Romania

1994 Kindergarten, East Windsor, New Jersey

1994 Anna Hospital Center, Bucharest, Romania

1994 Pontiac Dealership, Cranbury, New Jersey

1994 Credit Bank, Bucharest, Romania

1993 International Center for Film and Television, Bucharest, Romania

1991-1993 Industrial Export International Business Center, Bucharest, Romania

1992 Financial Administration Headquarters, Bucharest, Romania
(competition project)

1991 Community Transit Center, Venice, Italy
(competition project)

1990 West Hollywood Civic Center, West Hollywood, California
(competition project)

1990 Hemet Civic Center, Hemet, California
(competition project)

1989 Escondito Civic Center, Escondito, California
(competition project)

1989 University Square Office Building, East Windsor, New Jersey

1989 Swedish Mission to the United Nations,
New York, New York

1988 Coconut Grove Shopping Center Miami, Florida

1988 Allied Junction Development, Secaucus, New Jersey,
New Orleans Museum of Art,
New Orleans, Louisiana
(competition project)

1986 Alabama School of Fine Arts, Pennington, Alabama
(competition project)

1986 Theological Seminary Apartments, New York, New York

1985 Roger Williams College, School of Architecture Building
Providence, Rhode Island
(competition project)

1985 Hillsborough County Correctional Facility
Hillsborough County, New Hampshire

1984 Codex Headquarters, Massachusetts

1983-1984 Saks Fifth Avenue Tower, New York, New York

1983 Santa Barbara Museum of Art International Competition
Santa Barbara, California
(competition project)

1982 Iowa University Theater Addition, Iowa City, Iowa

1981 Miami Maritime Museum, Miami, Florida

1981 Paris Opera Competition, Paris, France
(competition project)

1980 West Point Chapel, West Point, New York

Professional Awards

Citation
1994 Progressive Architecture 41st Annual Awards Program
International Center for Film and Television Project; published in the January 1994 issue of Progressive Architecture

First Prize
1993 Mindbank Headquarters International

Competition Bucharest, Romania

First Prize
1992 Industrial Export International
Business Center International Competition
Bucharest, Romania

First Award
1990 High-rise Residential Development
Limited Competition
Frankfurt/Main, Germany

Award
1987 Escondido Civic Center International
Competition Escondido, California

1985 Roger Williams College School
of Architecture International Competition
Providence Rhode Island

1983 University of California at Santa
Barbara Museum of Art International
Competition Santa Barbara, California

Publications

L'Arca (Italy), April 1995
International Center for Film
and Television, Bucharest, Romania

Architectural Design (England),
November 1994
International Center for Film
and Television, Bucharest, Romania

Progressive Architecture, January 1994
International Center for Film
and Television, Bucharest, Romania

New York Architecture 1970-1990, 1990
Regatta Apartments, Battery Park City, N.Y.
Elizabeth Police Headquarters, Elizabeth, N.J.
University Square Office Building Princeton,
N.J.,
Rizzoli, New York

New York Architects 3, 1990
Seton Hall Law School, Newark, N.J.
Elizabeth Police Headquarters, Elizabeth
N.J.
West Hollywood Civic Center
West Hollywood, CA.,
U.S.A. Books, New York

L'Architecture D'Aujourdu'Hui (France),
February 1988
Elizabeth Police Headquarters
Elizabeth, N.J.

Architectura (Romania), May 1992
Industrialexport International
Business Center
Bucharest, Romania

Contraspazio (Italy), June 1993
International Center for Film and Television
Bucharest, Romania

Exhibitions
1993 Dae Jeon International Exibition
Dae Jeon, South Korea

1993 "Three Romanian-American Architects"
Romanian Mission to the United Nations
1992 "Romanian Architects Abroad"
Dalles Cultural Center,
Bucharest, Romania

1992 "Westfourth Architecture"
Institute of Architecture,
Bucharest, Romania

1991 "New York Architects"
Seoul, Korea

1991 Exhibition Installation For the Artist
Ion Banulescu
N.J.I.T. Gallery

1990 "New York Architecture 1970-1990"
Deutsche Archtektor Museum,
Frankfurt/Main

1990 "Faculty Exhibition," New Jersey
Institute of Technology

1988 " Architects for Social Responsibility"
Max Protech Gallery, New York

Education
1976 Master of Architecture
Institute of Architecture
Bucharest, Romania
1973 Bachelor of Architecture
Institute of Architecture
Bucharest, Romania

Professional Affiliations
American Institute of Architects
Union of Architects of Romania